MUSIC'S MASK AND MEASURE

JAY WRIGHT

Music's
Mask
and
Measure

FLOOD EDITIONS

CHICAGO

For permission, required to reprint or
broadcast more than several lines, write to:
Flood Editions, Post Office Box 3865
Chicago, Illinois 60654-0865
www.floodeditions.com

ISBN 0-9787467-3-2

This book was made possible in part
through a grant from the Illinois Arts Council

Design and composition by Quemadura
Printed on acid-free, recycled paper
in the United States of America

FIRST EDITION

Equation One

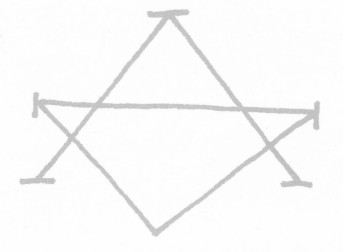

This ordinary language finds
rhythm in ambiguous flame,
that stable density of one
and one, the urgent displacement
that nurtures light.

Call it dancing in place,
a preparation
for movement, an impulse
that will awaken
a manifest order.

The astronomer has measured
the shadows. The resting body
measures its abrupt intention.
Who now has measured the waters
in the hollow?

Fall unveils the acute
aconitum, blue
light against the garden's
edge. You might hear
a greenish bird in flight.

Does water dream of seven green
saris, or of the melodic
inversion of sorrow, and will
episode and exposition
be love enough?

Return now to the hills
in balance, the field
of turbulent disguise,
the nothing that is,
the mountain's graceful scale.

*

Who would go into the river
to recover a seed, or sit
with a blacksmith and bard in high
lament? There is a universe
of such molecular intent
the water folds.

A cascade of bear at
this spot might bring us
justice, a particle death
and resurrection,
the ambivalent gift
from Artemis.

Seneca praised the conjugal
craft, the thread and disposition
equivalent to a young bride's
fortune, though he had never worn
the peplos nor sworn peace to a
troubled city.

Monday is diffident.
The rosebud ignores
its shy austerity.
But should this bubbling
authority now come
to a quiet end?

The anti-ascetic river
sets no limit upon the tau
or the attributes of lotus,
a water pot that holds the light.
Resignation comes hard on this
side of Being.

Equation Two

You will recall
the day the dead returned
            to the village.
Name it now
the nebula of perfect
expulsion.

These fragments
of existence spin their
enclosing
web, unlock
the uncertainty of grace.
We are late.

On the third day
we will dance with the beer;
the vessel will
be prepared
for the corrupted descent
of power.

Radiant
in its bounded estate,
the spirit
knows itself
as the guide who moves to erase
her footsteps.

So once again

the dance negotiates

the property

of being

strange, that absolute desire

for falling.

The red roof tiles
slip into the morning fog.
There is a red silence
      all around us.
It will take years to learn
this coherent grammar.

The oriole has established
an evasive coherence,
    infinite, exact,
with its place, there where
the day seems set to honor
the bird's expressive deceit.

Logic always
fails that Carolina wren.
The propositional
exactitude
of a certain absence
draws fire upon its wings.

The bird knows itself a strict
proposal of faith, a ground
state that moves without
an absolute space.
Grammatical bird, attuned
to roots and implication.

Love is ancient
evidence, an instrument
constrained, jealous of its
utility,
in awe of its own death;
every name embraces it.

Equation Three

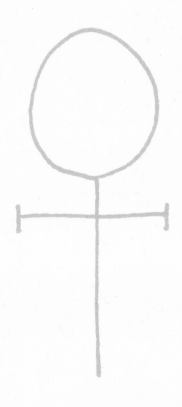

Completely disguised,
the dancer wears the mask
about his
body. This tree now falls,
a surface
and red lineage,

an axiom
and proposal,
the firm embrace
of the unsolved.

These are the elements
of desire:
black from the Dano
tree, the blood of a rock,
cattle bones
ground into whiteness,

and yellow clay.
Set to a new
measure, they form
their own release.

With wet snow
in the nearest birch,
October writes under
erasure.
Punch that for God's trace,
transcendental mistakes,

or the cozy
habitual
fire of harvest
free invention.

What we call
our own might only be
the first stroke upon
a stellar
clock, an instant shift
of center, a notion

the Cusan could
propose and stir
unfaithfulness
in the atom.

Never let it go.
Any instant can redeem
those objects
that distance can construct.
Or must we
misread existence

and the sly form
of a second
star, receding
and unremarked?

So God must surely die,
and heaven
be abandoned, each
system bled and given
to itself;
then you will draw your

conclusions by
natural light,
the infinite
physics of masks.

Equation Four

The fundamental measure
of this city
is not that bell tolling,
nor the tiled body that moves
as we move, resting here.

There you have us once again:
a supposition,
or transpositional
moment, chambered by our own
space, shadowed by our past.

That was an innocuous
moment, a strange
coordinate story.
Why should that enigmatic
gem be fundamental?

Bound by a complexity
of wave, the river
becomes a consonant
intrusion, the singular
flow of a constant point.

Silence structures a fragile
world; the little day
passes; darkness descends.
The expansive touch of prayer
makes love a random walk.

Copper is a vagabond,
a sea turtle,
the delirious eye
in the dance, and yet there is
a point to being whole.

The mask of cosmic design
dances alone,
with the vertical grace
of solitude; yet, pity
the burden of the frame.

An indiscretion would be
welcome, a flaw
in the calculation,
an ambiguous number
that frees a fine darkness.

What number fits the creative
exchange the star
disguises? A perfect
thermal equilibrium
astonishes belief.

Canons find entanglement
in caterpillars,
galaxies and balsam.
Death finds a spur in weaving
an ambrosial birth.

Deep in the earth's core, the judge
floats with the dead one.
We live with that figure
transcribed, the incarnation
that teaches air to flame.

Say at once that sumac seems
a fugitive
concern, a cellular
constellation that ignites
a second, sacred star.

Equation Five

The dune evening primrose
would be welcome here,
attuned to our silence.
Nothing here would shade
            its sere presence;
it would go down, searching
its strength and that welcome
disturbance called death.
We need, perhaps, a water birch,
with its scarred and reddish bark,
a native life that speaks to the rose
and draws us instantly home.

Sit
with the click and trill
of the broad-tailed hummingbird.
We have nestled,

         year by year,
in the traces of the same bird.
Yet, we might imagine
a skeptical bird,

         with its wings
embraced by the solar wind.
Count upon the scale of a burning bush,
or the perfectly habitable, silent tree.

This is the altar,

altered by a double desire.

Canonical hours call this curandero

out of his contradance;

he has learned to live with aberrant cactus.

Would Hilary praise him?

Would Paul open the door to his peculiar justice?

Only the dark matter of vision concerns him.

Step by rooted step,

the man will lead you to that other field

where nothing native belongs

and all is figure and blindness.

We have defined magmatic bliss
and an absolute luminosity
we will keep in our care.
       Resplendent logic
dresses our faith. If ruin
has a small beginning,
there is still the far-shining promise
       of a mortal altar
and a welcome dancer
who will not betray us.
Call this a surrounding fiction,
a transformative disposition.

All song is bent
by a silent measure;
a dancer's foot
is a luminous disk in flight.
This song is an open field,
and a fibrous exploration
          where the voice feels braced
by its own fluidity.
We will hope
that this dancer's body flows
with that expansive ambiguity,
all substance safe, all passion tempered.

*

Walking on East Palace,

those who sing find themselves oppressed

by juniper's shadow.

That sentence is logically true,

if, and only if,

the inoffensive crocodile remains

       a lexical substitution.

The answer lies in carbon-rich clay

and the thin significance

       of the insignificant body.

Say that this relational apprehension

has nothing to do with the world,

or the molecular complexity

of juniper's shadow,

and that the inoffensive crocodile swims

toward its lexical disaster.

JAY WRIGHT was born in Albuquerque, New Mexico in 1934 and spent his teens in San Pedro, California, where his father worked in the shipyards. After graduating from high school, he played for two minor-league ball clubs—Mexicali and Fresno —and spent a minute in spring training with the San Diego Padres of the old Pacific Coast League. He then served three years in the army, stationed in Germany. Thanks to the G.I. Bill, he received his B.A. in comparative literature from the University of California (Berkeley) and his M.A. from Rutgers University (New Brunswick). He has been a jazz and música Latina bassist and now lives with his wife, Lois, in Bradford, Vermont.

Wright is the author of eight previous books of poetry that were collected in one volume, *Transfigurations*, in 2000. He has also written more than thirty plays. A fellow of the American Academy of Arts and Sciences, his honors include a Guggenheim Fellowship, a Hodder Fellowship, a Lannan Literary Award for Poetry, a MacArthur Fellowship, and the Bollingen Prize for Poetry.